Window

Introduction

The collection of poems I accumulated over the years of the beauty of a life given to me through so many who came into my journey in my travels of life. May the love within these pages touch you in your heart like what fell before me in this world.

Copy write Robert Nacke

Soft Cover ISBN 978-1-387-29085-7

Biography

I was a little boy in a small town in the state of Illinois, where I grew up with my two sisters and one brother, with my Dad and Mom. My Dad is a gentleman who is a gifted carpenter, and my mother was a homemaker, raise us with love and happiness. I was a quiet child who had few friends, but no one near. In my school days, I took up a shop like all little boys, but, was shown far much more from my dear father, He taught me much more than a craft and using my hands, but the difference between right and wrong. I learned so much from my dear mother who taught me to be loving and kind to others. She also showed me the way around the kitchen and how one can survive on practically nothing by making a meal out of one thing. I love my parents so much because they showed me the values of life that I keep in my heart, always! The values I have learned made 2.

me a better person and I would [wouldn't] trade this for anything. My Mom is no longer here as she passed away from a serious ailment, which brings much sadness to me and my family. We all loved her so much! I know she is in a better place now and I know she is watching over me as my angel. I would not be who I am today without all the sacrifices both of them, my mother and father, made for me and my family, whom I love so much! I went through high school being a shy boy, only with a few friends, but no one near. At this time in my life, we moved back to a small town in the Midwest. I took up the art of woodworking that I learned from my loving Dad, who was a prominent teacher, as well. Time went on, I met people online who were writing and got me wanting to write by myself. I met one dear person who is always so sweet and caring. She gave me words of encouragements; that I am an excellent writer and she was proud of me. She is my guiding angel in life

3.

whom I love so much! Because of her, I found a way in writing. This blessed angel is my inspiration in all I do who is also an incredibly gifted writer, herself. I admire her so much in all she does!

My love has a unique way to express the beautiful world around us and shown me one can see far more when you look with your heart, then seen with eyes alone! I have one book of poems out with honorable mentions in a contest and I have a novel I wrote, a Fantasy romance, out, too. This collection of poems is a work over a period of years of a beauty of life I was blessed to witness.

Dedication

I wanted to dedicate this to my dear family first which I love so much and which gave me praises to continue in my writing, that I love doing so much! I also wanted to thank my dearest love in life who is my inspiration in all I do and told me I was a great writer. She said, never give up, as long as one believes in you feel it in your heart. I want to thank my love for helping me to write a poem in this edition called "under your Spell" and for a lovely writing she wrote, called "My Summer Love". I also want to dedicate this to my Lord Savior Jesus Christ, which none of this would be possible without him. He showed me such beautify in my life with such loving wonders I never take for granted; I am truly blessed being able to be here to see this in my life. I wanted also to thank my editor Christine Kaiser who is such talented lady and I also wanted to thank my cover designer Margo who did such a beautiful job on it that brought my vision of this book to life.

My Summer Love

As night turns into dreams and says goodbye to the day, we will again, tomorrow, see the light of the sun that God gave us; to feel the warmth, the love of life, just, like our love that melts like the magical night into the light from the stars that shower us with love - that embraces our souls like one. You and I are the songs of life. A dance that never ends when our eyes meets I see myself in yours. When I feel my heart beat, I know it's your heart that beats in a rhythm from past, long before we met. You were already holding me in your warm embrace. When you whispered, I love you, from that moment in time - I knew that I loved you more.

Angels

In this world, there is something so wonderful going [on?] - we call it life, my friends. You cannot taste it or touch it, yet, it is very moving to see, as there are angels here in this world. I am talking about those extraordinary acts of kindness and loving for all! People say there are no such things out there, but I say boulder dash to that. I see it happen each and every day, right here among us all. From the friendly gesture of a simple hello or, even the concern of their fellow man, as it does happen. They have no wings or halos, yet they inevitably fly so high with their loving acts, where their halos shine so brightly! The good Lord has blessed me with many angels in my life. At first, glance, when I met this dear soul, I knew were an angel, those face I see is so kind; and after knowing you, I can say you are my friend and will always be. Your sweet and loving ways have changed me for the better. I have more respect and kindness to others because of all of you. You are and forever will be my angel friends!

9.

Angels Eyes

There is a beauty showing a soul that cast love; it is one from a man from Heaven to see. The reflecting pool of beauty, that stands before one's heart. You look upon these blessed eyes of beauty to see - an image of the love of two people that cast a glow of radiant beauty in all life. It is one dearest soul that has ever been here on earth. An Angel shows the beauty of your heart so openly. It is like she sees your heart that is a window to who you are in this life, a man wanting to find one who is sweet and caring at heart, who is a blessed angel here in this life. She has no wings, yet she surely flies in all beautiful glory! Her eyes have cast off the shackles that bound your heart, which is; at last, free to show the beauty of my heart. These beautiful eyes always show love, always! My angel is such a dear heart who radiates love that warms me even within the cold winter winds of life. The dear one of my, hear is a real angel, who shown me Heaven here on earth. There are many saying, there is no such thing as angels here on earth o, that there is no Heaven, but they never had a true love like this. Love is now, you see it clearly in the eyes of an angel that has no wings to fly, yet she has soared into my heart for all eternity!

11.

Angel's Love

There is a love so deep and special, showing you the beauty of one's soul. The lord Savior shows you a fine wonderful love that is sweet and caring. You see the beauty of her soul that stands out like a beacon from a lighthouse, shining its beam of light to keep ships safe in the darkness of the sea. You know this angel is such a beautiful soul, that you will love forever! Fate was at work because; you know it was the good Lord, who blesses one another with the greatest treasure of life - which is love. You started out as friend, sharing the same things of life but, as your friendship grew you see this dear one is the most blessed soul that you have ever met! You see this most caring woman as the one you can share your life with, always! No matter what! She would never put you down in what you say. She will listen to you, always and I tell you, it sounds terrific - that it should be tried – and it will be your great success! An Angel has shown you many things of beauty, that has made you feel blessed by her, always. She inspires you daily, which is what gives you the courage to try things out, you never thought could be done. One lovely beauty of divine goodness has made you a better man. She has shown you all that those others, have such caring souls in them. You look at your dear sweetheart angel, you love so much, seeing a caring woman who is like your heart and soul! Sweet princess is such a ray of sunshine, always giving you love that warms you heart. My blessed angel's voice is like hearing a choir singing, as if one was in Heaven, which leaves me speechless! The beauty seen before me, is my angel who is my future; who brings greatness out of me in life, we are sharing here today. My heart is moved by this because, an angel's love is with me forever!

Beautiful Day

God has shown us much beauty here on this earth. The beautiful sunrise on a perfect day where all looks so grand. The vision of God has given so much; we can all see his beautiful creations in the way he wanted us to see. You see his loving hand each day when you see a glorious sunset in the sky, especially when there is not a cloud in the heaven, but the brilliant shades of red on the horizon, like you can reach out to hold it in your hands! Those who see God's beauty, like a majestic bald eagle gliding the heaven, is seeing them in all the beauty of life, as they take care of their offspring is indeed moving. Now, that is a breathtaking moment that would swoon even a grown man to come to tears. That is, when you see all his glory he gives us. Even on a lake, where the reflection is pristine as if one is looking into a mirror. When people see such beautiful things how can they not believe in God, or say so when they see it with their own eyes - his beauty here on this earth! His love for us is robust and everlasting. Our Father does not judge anyone, for he loves all his children, always! The real love of our Lord Savior is there, where he shows the beauty within, always from his heart to ours. The sun is shining brightly in its beautiful ray of light, as God is kissing his everlasting love on all of us. His loving light begins its new day in the warm haze that will bring peace to the most troubled soul on this sea of his harbor. One, which you will never see storms there; it is always paradise to all who opens their heart to it. The beautiful birds of love are chirping an ever beautiful song of life, bringing wonderful melodies to all who hears them. They are happy to sing to all those who love them in all the natural glory in their sound of love. They feel the beauty of our Lord savior's blessings that is granted us what we are living here today. The beauty we see all around shows his love so well. If you just take the time to see his love, that is placed before of us! There are so many out there who do not take the time to feel his beautiful gift from the heart, that has so much within in his excellent message, if you just take the time to hear - that today and every day is a great day that is worth living here and now!

Under Your Spell

When lovers hearts, beats into the dark of the night where only the lit candle flickers the way in the eyes of passion.
The, a warm embrace tenderly seeking lips entwine, when the eye of the soul shower the stars of desire. When lovers hearts, beats under the spell from the moon. Their hearts sings the song of lasting forever, written on the stone of life they share as one. Beautiful do they look when they joined from the first moment - two hearts touches, because, from that time they knew without a doubt, that this is love and there is, nor will ever be any other whose hearts will sing of the beauty they share here on earth.

Love

There is sadness that moves around us here in this world like a pooling water fountain in a park that spurts a stream of despairing anger with no beauty within our hearts. Earth, the majestic planet we call home, has seen its share misery in its adolescence of year; she saw the beauty that comes from the heart of life, with love for others. It is truly breathtaking to behold here today. Many think this is a dream, that there is no humanity of love out there for others anymore. They need to look what is before them, though not with eyes alone, as one need to look with their heart that sees far more than with eyes alone. We must learn with wisdom, there is far more beauty with love then there is with hate. Everyday kindness to others is truly beautiful and who give this to others, are angels here on Earth. Yes, they are angels, though they have no wings. Their compassion to those around

18.

them makes their halos shine brightly! The beautiful kindness of others can be a loving act. Just saying hello shows more strength then thrashing outward with a striking blow of anger. Hate is like quicksand, the more you struggle with it the faster you sink into it and despair in your sorrows. Love is a beautiful virus, that spreads quickly all around. That needs no cure because, life will always be beautiful with it, here and now!

Beautiful Lady

One sees all things in life like the beautiful sunset, that has shades of brilliant yellows, making one think of a smile who lights the whole sky. The hue of orange you find on a tree that comes from the sun shining, caress you with the surrounding beauty and brings the essence of an angel you love to you. My dearest heart beauty is far more than what can be seen with eyes alone, as her heart takes my breath away, always! The dear heart will always share the blessings of life with me that God has bestowed upon us here in life. She paints so beautiful on this canvas of life, she is like Michael D'Angelo who creates a masterpiece that is timeless. Love has drawn me to this amazing woman that I have met. She has so many blessed gifts; she received from our dear Lord Savior Father, which one is her caring for others. I see her so beautifully act, without hesitation, to help someone in need. This moves me to tears, her selfless act of kindness. The beauty of life she shares with me takes my breath away by what we hold in our hearts, that never fad [Fades]; like a flower that withers in a garden – though, our love will remain vibrant, full and always with beauty within our hearts. I feel deep in my heart, love. We share an eternal flame that is burning brightly for all; to see what we have is a beautiful blessing of life, living always! Many are not willing to see that when you share love with someone, it is a cosmic union that is written across the vast stream of two people, who are destined to meet and fall deeply in love. Sure it is easy to turn your back on love, because they are angry, thinking they are unworthy for such beautiful thing, but love is truly worth it! If all saw this, it would be a far better place to be. Love has drawn me to the most amazing woman that I ever knew. She has so many blessed gifts she received from our Lord, which one of them is her caring for others. I have seen her so beautifully act without hesitation help someone in need. The aura of love that is in he, is one I never tired of looking. I hold her soft hands tenderly and look her in her beautiful eyes so blue, though no words we speak, it is what we knew in our hearts. It is a blessing that remains forever. The first moment God bless me with my angel has been the happiest since I been here on earth! There are times when love is profound and strong; no word can say how you are feeling, and when all you need is to be near your heart in life. I look into her eyes to see our love surely; she painted on a canvas for all to see! Our love will be one that all will see as true everlasting because my love, my beautiful lady, is my angel from Heaven who is my life here on earth.

Beauty of God

God has shown us much beauty here on earth. From the beautiful sunrise, on a perfect day, where all looks so grand; when you cannot tell where the land and heavens of the sky begin with a breathtaking moment that moves all who sees the gift of life. We can see all his beautiful creations in the way he wanted to, so we can share his love he bless us each and every day in life we are living one in heart and soul. Those who sees who sees our loving Fathers beauty takes for granted what is bestowed upon us like a robin singing on a new spring day to an eagle soaring the blue heavens of life in being free to live life, as it was meant to be, is a real blessing to cherish always! There is much to be treasured in one's heart like seeing your children grow in life to be all they can be is such a beautiful moment that brings you to tears by this. The beauty of God comes to all of us each day in various ways that take our breath away in life. As these moments come, how can one not believe in our Lord Savior Jesus Christ with their own eyes? His love for us is robust and everlasting, where he does not judge his children. He loves us for who we are in our hearts, where the beauty of God will remain in time today, tomorrow, and for all eternity!

Beauty of All

For the beautiful soul of a loving heart, for she is this lovely woman who is your true love now and forever. There is not a second goes by that you do not think of this dear beautiful heart of a woman. You find yourself waking in the early hours of a day thinking of your love and the life; you will soon be sharing together. Thinking of her, you find the hours have passed, where it seems mere minutes has come. You want to be with your princess, always. To share the beauty of life together. Some may think this is a fool in love, but, I say no to that this is a love, so strong in a bond, that even time spans itself! You show her love each day, so this angel will know she has been loved always! My angel will know no tear will fall from her, as long as we are one in life. Her love is forever as I see it each moment, joined from her words she writes, she is truly beautiful from her heart to mine that is forever! My dearest heart knows my love is true in all I share with her and would trade all for an eternity with me. Ours is joined in heart and soul for an eternity, which evens this length of time, can express our love that can never fade away!

Soul Love

The light soar across the space of time with the essence of a life of two joined from the first embrace of living here on earth. Hearts hears the song of beating in pure harmony, shared of two, who are meant to be one for all eternity! The sweet melody moves seamlessly in the beacon of life, warming the heavens with a lasting light above. Stars light the darkness in a warm ray of love that they share across the stream of time. Lips share kisses that warm dearly in hearts with sensations from their head to toes. Moments they share are pictures of a perfect life that seems too quick, though the love they share is an eternity because their souls are entwined with love today, tomorrow, and for all eternity!

My Love

Love,

Light of Heaven do I see across the ocean, you with me as God meant it to be. Our love is a burning flame in the dark that sparks from the start, with songs playing on a harp that never will part. Hands of you and me I feel of love, where we soar above like two doves. Passing of time, chimes of songs, of two hearts, that will be forever. Long of life we share be it night or day. The beauty I see brings me to tears, knowing you are showing me love from your heart. From the start that will never part. Words of three from you to me set me free, because I LOVE YOU eternally!

One

One heart is beating its life to me.
One angel sings sweetly in rhythm with lost time.
One song heard from a dear bird, who flown from yours to my heart from the start.
One dance of love moves me to you, who is my soul in life.
One kiss we share moves in my heart, flying in the air from the start.
One tear falls, because you are with me in years of eternity.
One life we share with true love above, where we soar like doves.
One moment with you is not passing time for the hour chimes for an eternity.

His Love

Rejoice -Our Father comes once more to life with a love he always shares to all! Days of gloom felted with the crucifixion, but he said, „fear not my children I will raise for you with love!" That day he was laid to rest with sadness, but those who believed with love in their heart, knew he would come to them once more. As time passed, the stone rolls away, where they look in to see our Lord is not there. His children feel his love in their heart that brings joy to all who believe in him. Love comes again throughout all time because our Savior lives in our hearts always! The blessings of life are felt by all in days of beautiful because our God has risen for us with his love that we share today, tomorrow, and for all eternity!

Awaking

Heart quiet time in the darkness of hours of life, feels hands of; calls out in a sweet voice of an angel from Heaven here on earth. The sweet harmony sings of a life of love, playing the song of two whose hearts were meant to be. A face I do see moves me dearly by the beauty I see; within a heart who brings me life, completely! For so long in the past, the veil of darkness kept my heart from seeing what was there. From the moment a dear angel, is when I saw the beautiful dawn of life, appeared before me when hands caress tenderly of warm love. The veil moves away from my heart's closing eyes to reveal the beauty I have been missing here in the hours of life when I look at me, to see one who means more to me than life itself. For Destiny told me of a love of you and me, where it was inscribed for all to see, what real love means, that is forever in you and me. The dark heart is no more, for the awakening came to - and never will be again because the union of love is today, tomorrow, and for all eternity!

Fields of Love

The breath of life blows gently on the plains, swaying the lovely green blades of grass moving to the beautiful song playing in the hours of life. The sunlight caresses two hearts, warming the heavens. They are blessed being one in the union of lasting love.
As the light surrounds them in a glow, they embrace tenderly; feeling their hearts beat in a perfect harmony of lasting forever! They kiss tenderly of love, as their eyes meet, where they see the beauty they painted from the first moment when God created them from Heaven here on earth. The light shines brightly from them, as their souls entwine across the field. They are lying on in the fields of love that they know will keep growing today, tomorrow, and for all eternity! The divine love they share is such moving site to

behold by all who sees, who are truly in love. Deeply in there. It is the most beautiful for one and all

Love of Thee

My love, as stars from Heaven shines on thee who means to me more than the air I breathe. Hark for the spark of a harp playing in my heart.

Of Love that thee brings to me, setting us free, forever be. All along songs belong within you and me. Eyes of blue from you do not make me sad for they show love above forever thee. Hearts entwine in time shine in the dark from the start. Lips of thee set me free, where we soar forever more above with love.

Blessed By All

Everyone comes in touch with people in their lives though some are a just brief passing moment, this changes you in a way that only God could have made happen. Everyone is affected by this monumental life changing event because these encounters are with angels of our Lord Savior that can be only better you as person. You do not notice it right in your life, but these life changing events goes into your heart and soul. It all starts with two most blessed angels that brought you to life in this world; those dear souls are your Mom and Dad. They mold you into the person you are today who taught you what is good in life. There are even those who treated you badly and did you wrong though this has happen they are blessings to you. They help you to see there is so much good out there, which is a small stepping stone in your life. You meet people when you are in school that changes you dramatically! Then from someone who will be your friend, who you will laugh, play and even cry and are a blessings from Heaven here on earth. Some teachers will help you also in life, where they give their vast knowledge that opens your eyes to a new world out there. We may not always see them as ones who have blessed us. But surely they have blessed us as God does. There is one life to change moment that affects all when you meet someone and fall madly in love. The connection with your dear love is so deep and profound that you never want to leave as all moments are precious to you. My angel shows me so much beauty out there in life that brings you tears by what showed of life that you know will never end. You love her with all your heart that keeps growing stronger as time moves across the vast universe. There are many you meet in life that has this profound effect upon you that shapes you into the man you are today. These lessen never ends in your life; the school never rings dismissal because we will always meet those who bless us all!

When you are soon by my side

I hear your voice from far away I cling to the memories of our love

I am in search for your love; please love me my shining light my only one.....

The beating of my heart thunders across the storm swept horizon, calling forth the sweet melody of love that will never be silence within my soul. Sing to my dreams of soft whispers to my mind where only you and I will find.

The magic of heaven when we touch I will feel you again from the moment you are mine.....Lips of sweetness I feel when we kiss in a longing desire as the night closes in on us in a beauty that we hold in our hearts that is one. For this blessing we shared is one that never will fade away like a bad dream that bumps into the night. Warm surrenders of love flow from my head to my toes when you are soon by my side, for you and I are one forever!

Friends Legacy

We all are destined to a legacy that one's action affects all who sees it in our existence in our life. Everyone who has ever walked this high life in our universe has a lasting effect on someone. You need not have to climb a highest peak of a mountain or swim the biggest ocean or even be a famous world leader. We all have a great preordained plan lay before them. It is one blessed thing of all who sees this. It is one of a friendship of people in your life that you have a particular connection. You start out as strangers meeting in a crowded building and have a small talk. You see then those blessed souls with the same interest in things in life, but for the most part, it is what you felt in your heart. The one person that you can confide in to tell them your troubles which will listen and try to reassure you through your problems there is a friend and always is. Your friendship grows in your heart and theirs like a beautiful flower that grows in God's love that never will fade away. You see their heart so clearly that adds beauty in your life where one sees the good that is there always! These dear souls who we call friends are the ones who have blessed us so much. It is love, the caring that shows you there are pure angels here on earth. They have no wings, yet their halos shine brightly. Their caring reflects of all who stands before them in life. The blessing that come forth is a start of something that is so beautiful, those dear ones who you call friends. They think they are not important in your life. But I say they are wrong. Because, they are kissed by God, himself. If they only open their hearts and see that it is all around them in life. They will see this is a beautiful, blessed illness, one where we need no cure because, it is one spread by a love of one's heart in this sea of life. The dear angels we call friends has helped to shape who we are today in life. They show us the beauty of all around us is the blessing from God who wants all his children knows he loves them. One of the greatest things one can hold in his heart is this legacy friendship. So let us keep this going on. Let us pass the torch always, where the flame never dies!

Christmas Spirit

Christmas is a great time of year, which always brings out the best in everyone. The time of year, where you see grown men act like kids in a candy shop, savoring over the sweets in a display. You can be out walking down a street during this blessed time of year and see two complete strangers take the time to say Merry Christmas to one another. Like any other time, people rather pass you by without even saying Hi. During this time of year you go by a dark, lonely street, where you hear in the distance a most beautiful Christmas hymn. We listen to this beauty that makes us emotional because, we think of our pass of the love we have for our family. The greatest Christmas spirit is Santa Clause who is always full of good cheer for us all, even when most do not believe in him anymore.

He is always full of love and good cheer who cares for us all. Old St. Nick is the spirit of the good Lord himself because; his love is everlasting for all! Christmas is Gods way of bringing us happiness in our lives, even if it is for a short time; yet, may this love at Christmas will spread worldwide and last all year. We all have this Great Spirit in each of us. If only we had the wisdom to let it show throughout and not worry what others will say if we let it show. The beautiful spirit of Christmas need not to vanish, so, instead we need to celebrate it. Let the glory of love shine in your heart not just at Christmas, but each and every day.

Destine to Be

There is a love that is fated in your life, when you love the woman of your dreams who is forever in me. From the moment God inscribed the loving words from my heart, I felt our hearts joined across the cosmos where we sail the Heavenly bounds hand in hand for all eternity. My angel came across the sands of time with a key she placed in my heart that unlocks, where before I was waiting for her; who is my soul forever, as it was meant to be. I see the future so clearly, where we are living day after day, together as one; where we can feel the blessings God has gave us. Love, that we will always cherish in our hearts. The love we share will never become cold in our hearts because, what we hold inside of one another keeps growing stronger day after day. For our love is destiny to be, as it was inscribed here in life we shall and always live joined in heart and soul!
45.

Deep Love

There is love so strong and so unique in one's life that you want all to feel the way you are feeling now! A Love, that you feel in your heart, as if no other love can. One blessed woman of your life shows you all the beauty of life that is deep inside your heart. You know this love is one of heart and not of lust. Everything she does, or says to you is truly beautiful. My heart races in excitement at this sweet love that stands before me. My dear angel holds the key to my heart that was for so long locked away, until fate came and brought us together, as it was meant to be. My angel is my soul mate who I have a deep connection to because; I feel her deep inside my heart that is always singing about everlasting love. If someone were to look up the definition of most beautiful, the answer would be: this dear lady, of my heart. I feel her in all walks of life like the wind blowing in my face that could be her sweet kisses from afar; and the sun warming me in the winter's cold and that warms me with her arms of loving life we are living here today. As all I experience, I know without a doubt God himself sent me his sweet angel who I love so much! Our love is the greatest in all there is and most beautiful, because ours is a deep love that is one we hold firmly in our hearts that joins from the moment life began here on earth.

Love to Me

Love to me,

Came one day when the cloud of loneliness filled me with the cold rain of life. Angel sun of happiness moved across the miles when my real love in life flew into my heart with warm caress, I have never known until that moment. Eyes of blue I see with a forever lasting joy; we will know each day that we will experience in every precious moment, we will treasure always! Beauty in life I want to know with my dearest angel from Heaven. Where we can hold hands in the quiet waking of a new day being set forth to us and the end of a day we lay close to see the closing of our day, where we give thanks to our Lord Savior who bless us so much in our lives. I want to grow old with my love, to see the gracious beauty of the one that is my heart. Beautiful she is each day, where I look upon her to have my heart race like a herd of stallions running free through the fields of life! Love, to me is falling in love with one like it was the very first time, as my heart has, nor will love no one but you. The life I feel now, because love joined in our hearts that will never fade like the sun at the end of the day. Love, live it always in one's heart, for without there is no hope.

Face of a Angel

Calls of Heavens grace on those in needs, in no words needed to speak, for words from the heart is clearly. Love sows its beauty when you set forth on one who has completely capture your heart. You see this blessed angel as the most beautiful caring soul ever; you need not see wings because surely flown right into your heart! Heaven cast a perfect glow of beauty that is of this dear angel from God. She moves me for all she does in this life, takes my breath away by what she bless me with. For so long my heart has been locked in chains, that would not fall away until an angel came to me, holding the key that removes this iron prison of 50.

darkness. Never, joy was felt for another, until this dear heart came across the sands of time with the warmth of love that was meant to be. No words can say what I am feeling inside for my dear love in life, because all that is said, spoken from my heart to hers that never will be silenced! Our love is one from the ages of life that puts in place on the path for love is our destiny for all eternity! I look upon my sweetheart to see the beauty of her soul of my heart, where I see the face of an angel who is my forever guiding light of the heart that is beating only for one.

God Sent

There is that certain someone who comes along in your life that you almost immediately connect to in all in life. You start out as strangers meeting in passing on a street or in a crowded room and then with a simple hello you start wondering if this person could be someone you want to know better. You start this beautiful friendship by exchanging things about your lives to one another and finding things you love about each other. From the way one talk or their funny little laugh that you find so darn inviting; plus how they hold their own in the face of the difficulty of life. You find in each passing days the more you know this blessing one 52.

conclude that you care for them so much! From the first moment when this beautiful relationship began it felt, you see them your whole life. Though the time you knew each other has been short in human years, unlike a beautiful bald eagle that mates for life. Our love is truly beautiful and forever unique like no other because when you find one who is God sent, that is what holds you in one another heart's is a precious gift that never will be let go.

Goddess

My is a woman who shines every day with the radiant beauty of her heart and soul, a sweet loving woman whose real beauty is in how she treats others in life. Many men lust for the physical attraction to a woman and do not see there is so much more than what one sees by eyes alone. A man, who sees a woman's heart, knows a real goddess and though this is true quality like no other, her beauty takes one's breath away! She graces the heavens with love for her God, the one true man that sees beyond her gorgeous body, yet she knows he is here for her just waiting to be loved by his dearest heart. Her God, who wants to be with his goddess, knew she was different than 54.

others he saw before from the sweet caring hold she shares in all she holds in life. The two of them has changes in their lives that would be considered sad, is when fate steps in to help them to see their life of forever love! From that moment these dear hearts are truly happy because they will live this sea of life until the heavens are no more!

Beautiful Star

Beautiful star where art Thar? From a far there you are shining brightly that fills like a jar in who you are. Five points of Heaven do I see of thee who move me completely. Beauty I see when I look at thee who sets my heart with glee when you are near me. Eyes of blue shows true of you with love up above that we fly high in the sky. Love is for told when we hold that is more precious than time. Beautiful star shine like a dime for you have won my heart from the start that never will part.

56.

Heaven's Love

An angel is dancing so gracefully across the huge Milky Way, to soar the sky for all to see. You see a falling star in the dark span of the heavens that is an angel showing the beauty of life that is wrapping up in love of one's heart. The beauty of love that is needed in all of us when life seems bleak is bathing by divine hands placed within our showers the warm glow of lasting love that places in our hearts for all time to come. Beautiful it is when two souls meet as determine by the call of Heaven and set in motion the clock of love in hearts that bring forth feelings of lasting happiness in all! You look towards the heavens and what do

57.

, but an angel whose beauty is   and so sweet. You gaze into her beautiful eyes of blue that show her loving soul that opens your window of heart with love always. The future you see standing before you hand in hand, sharing life's moment that is fragments of time flowing in our hourglass that will never cease to flow for lovers whose hearts are one for all time.

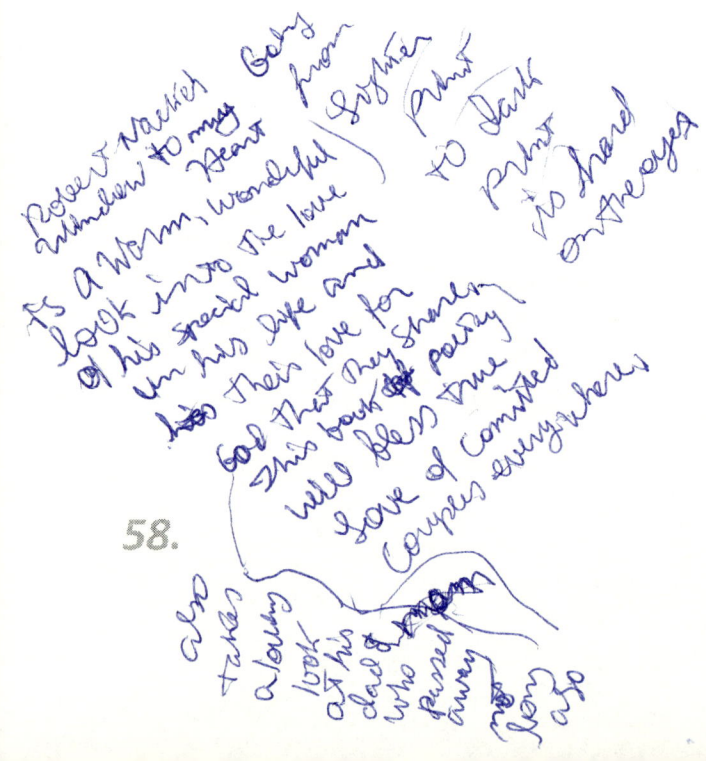

Heart Felt

There are many feelings one has in life, such as feelings of happiness like if you win a lottery that makes them wealthy. You also feel sadness if you lose your dear parents that brought you into this world, feeling the anguish that one was not there when they needed you the most. Then there is the feeling of love that is most beautiful of all the feelings one can have in life! Many search their entire life looking for such a person to share with always. When one finds such a person in life, it happens without a warning as it resides deep in your heart. No one can tell of love because it is what you feel in one's heart of a lasting blessing when two

comes together as it was meant to be. As when it happens to you, it is a beautiful moment that sends warm sensation upon you when your angel says I love you. Look into her eyes, which are stunning that moves you beyond words by what you see because her eyes are the window to her dear loving heart and sweet soul of Heaven here on Earth. There are so many in lives that are always looking for the one because they think there is another who is better as they fail to see the beautiful flower before them. They think there is a thorn before them that will hurt one instead thereof the rose that is truly beautiful that is always heartfelt for those who are soul loves that will always be one today, tomorrow, and for all eternity!
60.

Home in the Heart

People may say home is a structure with four walls and a roof though made from wood and plaster. Yes, it gives us shelter from the elements and it gives us warmth when it is cold or protects from the driving rain that breeds life in all Gods creations. These does have a life of its own from the souls who put their heart in it to make it whole, yet it cannot love a person when they are sad or even praise them for having a great day. Home is in the heart of all who is living in life. We all are very essence of a life of a real home, because we breed life into the very foundation that lies. A house is a building with four walls and a roof, but it cannot love you as a mother who loves her child when in pain. Then, what about a man, who cannot see though by good grace from God who brings a miracle of sight to look upon his family he loves so much. Then there is an angel who knows her hearts love will spend his life loving only her because he sees her as the most amazing woman in all the world! They will raise a family together, out of the love they feel in their hearts beating as one. It is sad many will never know this beautiful feeling of love and being with those who you care for, which they only know greed of life in the search for the glitter of gold. They never see that when you have a family that this is the real home in the heart.

62.

I Do

*When two are so much in love, they long to hear words that are so beautiful in nature, because when one says them, it starts a path of life-long commitment into your heart. The blessing you received from one another is ever beautiful like a rainbow that appears from the heavens after a summer shower; it is lovely as seeing two who joining as one in life. These are the words all who are in love wants to hear. As when this man and this woman stand together before **God** and all hand in hand when they share their love with words that flow beautifully from hearts that sings in perfect harmony. One blessed angel, you see standing before* *you is a real princess who truly is so beautiful that you know you are meant to be with her for eternity. My sweet princess is my angel, blessed by God who shown me his greatest angel. The love we share is a magical gift we hold close in our hearts. As our love came, it seems like time moves slow as if one is moving through quicksand that stops you in your journey in an instant! Love is one that will be forever, which many may take for granted. Because those who do not see this beautiful experience as a precious gift from another, which they think love is only a feeling of lust or even just one day of the year. But it is a commitment in the heart of two coming together. Two in love say from their heart two words that will 64.*

always be beautiful. It is more than just speaking them; it is feeling them. When you are truly in love, as I do, it is an incredible feeling for your heart that is beating for only one.

Mountain of Love

Peaks and valleys run through the green lush paths of life like our hearts, that sows love we planted. Time aged the soil dug in the rich path of life's journey, together hand in hand with blessings from our Lord Savior who sets us on this beautiful path. With blue skies we see the precious stone, love, that we created by our hearts that is on top of the mountain of love that never will wither away to the plain of sadness crying on the lost highway of life.

66.

Life

You came into this world, not with care. You start out as someone's greatest love and joy who were your loving parents who gave you life and attention in this world. They show things of life that will make you a better person, which you pass along to others you meet in the hours of time in sharing kindness is a beautiful legacy from them that is most beautiful. You are the person you are today because of them, who shows that is far more beautiful to give then take with cruelty in one's heart and that

67.

every action there is an equal reaction to what comes in life. There is then a particular time in one's life that you will meet someone that will come to you in this life that will be such an important part of it!

At first, there is an attraction to them by physical appearance; then, as you get to know this sweet loving soul, one sees there is so much you have in common with her. You see this is the one you love with every fiber of your being! You find yourself thinking of the beautiful soul of your life every second of the day and realize this is your soul mate who *you want to spend your life with in all moments of time. There is such a wonderful aura of her being that moves you deeply in your heart and you know without a doubt that no one can break this love you are feeling today because this is true love and life that is worth living with my one and only love*

Alone no more

Listen to the stillness all around when the echoes of time beats, beats to the heart of life. Living in the emptiness in the dark womb of a void that coldness shivers in the blowing, howling wind into your bones for being alone is known to hold, to keep me in a veil of sadness that makes me feel bad. The dark shroud covers the light of joy in life, a life that seems not worth living. As I look up to Heaven, I prayed for light to come to that answers again when my angel, came to me. From that moment God answer 70.

me with you, the dark cloak was removed to show the warm sunshine above, warming sands we are standing on life's shores. Beauty I see standing with me, hand in hand, with love, beautiful love we share throughout all time. Gift of love we treasure in our hearts that is cherished deeply and from that moment God sent me my angel I knew that I am alone no more with you in my heart for all eternity!

71.

Today Love

The heart beating life, lasting life to me is one soul whose heart sings of Heaven here on Earth. Hands of my and yours caress of warm tenderness, where I see our story unfold of the beautiful beginning when we met to write a story that continues this moment. We are living in a love story that never has The End. Words spoken of love, the beautiful words coming from our hearts that says so well what we are feeling even when no words are needed. Our eyes look with a warm tenderness of love to see a soul whose future is for them from the moment life came to be. Because this was when we knew it was our destiny that was for told of this moment standing together hand in hand. For today love we have that will last today, tomorrow and for all days to be for as one is beautiful always in life.

Love

Love is an eternal beauty of one's soul; it spreads warm feelings from the heart in all, who bask in its ever essence of love's sweet scent like a beautiful flower sharing its sweet fragrance. Love is so lovely, as they are your ray of the sunshine from your heart that never will set. One in a heart is your dearest soul mate who is an angel whose beauty is truly breathtaking inside and out! My angel loves me so, as much I love her with each breath I take. A life that breathes in from an air of love we share always! The way of the heart has no time when one is truly in love as you would wait an eternity for the one that is so deeply in your soul. Feeling of love is not control by your head, but by your heart. Yes at times it makes you do foolish things, which may look silly though it matters not when in love. There is many beautiful things happen when you are in love from sharing a beautiful sunrise at the beginning of a new day to seeing your love smile when you tell her how beautiful she is. My angel shows me all in life is achievable, where all is possible as long as you never lose hope for when in love can be reach by two who believes in each other. We all have experienced this in our lives, which some deny this because they are afraid of being close, fear of being hurt if they are wrong. Those who are scared of this never will know that there is beauty in being in love by one is a real gift that can and always will sharing of two beautiful souls who are forever!

Love by an Angel

There is a love that is strong and so beautiful in life that is known so well, because of one sweet angel in your life. You look at the beautiful night heaven and count the stars in the sky with the point of light by them is a beacon shining down for the most beautiful in all the world! There are not enough stars to say how deep my love goes because it is an eternal flame that never runs out of life here in this vast universe we are living as one. My dear angel and I are two hearts that beats as one in perfect uniform harmony that sings a love that never is silence. Every moment we share in life, is an incredible journey, traveling on the road we are sharing all together with her is a blessing from God who

76.

shown me Heaven here on Earth. My love, my angel, is my one who is my soul mate whose love I hold in my heart and give her my love a thousand times over, because there has, nor will be no other but her. Many who may see this as a foolish dream to be in love with someone I would say they are wrong, because they do not know what real love is until truly loved by an angel.

Life Is Beautiful

Life is the most blessed thing, it is rosy and bright like a beautiful girl in pigtails, as when you see this just melts your heart. You just feel good seeing this dear child who brings so much joy to those all around. Life all around is full of many blessings that make one stop to take in this beautiful gift God has bestowed upon us that is a treasure that can never lose its worth. The richest men in the world can never be truly happy like those, who has no material value because, they are so busy in seeking a beautiful gem that they fail to see the precious jewel of life is in one's heart, in sharing to others. For so many who feel that to be rich and the need of fancy cars, or things of gold or, even shining jewels that sparkle like beacons showing those around your value, but if you have no one to share your heart with what good does all your wealth is worth in the world. The one who has the way of the heart is more valuable that even the wealthiest man on Earth cannot put this in his wallet. When you have a love of your Lord, your real love and family, friends makes life truly beautiful. There is nothing better than this day, when one then can say life is beautiful and is worth living today, tomorrow and all days moving in time worth living today, tomorrow and all days moving in time.

I Love You

Three magical words are dear to your heart that most people lose track of the actual meaning of it in life. These three words I love you is the most beautiful words anyone can hear in their life. It means one's true feelings from the heart that only two people, who have found each other. It is not lust or desire that sparks this blessed flame that burns! These feelings run deep that shows what God placed in your heart forever! You see your dear heart that ignites you into words of beauty. It is when you look in their eyes and see the love, they have for you, is one remarkable feeling in the world! It is much more, so when given by the one who holds your heart for all time; it is even more special when you 8o.

hear it from your dear angel! When this sweet caring that who is truly beautiful said I love you is a moment you will never forget. One moment like this will forever etch into your heart; it is a wonderful feeling that makes one feel alive and blessed by God himself. As being loved by someone is like seeing a beautiful spring day in all its glory of flowers showing their beauty like your blessed angel is always! One knows that it is a life of love from this dear soul who came into your life that will be filled with joy that is worth living, because of her your sunshine from Heaven here on earth. I look into her dear eyes that are the window to her sweet, caring soul, where she generously open to me, showing me a future that we will share always! Life began the 81.

moment these three beautiful words spoken from one who warms the heart completely because I love you is always felt in the heart and will never die because love is the beautiful flame burning brightly for all to see.

Love just for one

When one is in Love that is so profound and vigorous! It is Love that is the most beautiful of all. You feel a certain connection that is a warmly blessed feeling that is beautiful in life! You know this love you have here is one that you know, she is the one for you in your life that will be with you always; this love of your Life is one that you need by your side. Because, when you are apart, you feel like an endless black hole that never has a place to end. Feelings like this are the same when you are away from your beloved; yet, even though apart, you know your love will survive. You both know there is a lifetime of togetherness in the two! You are, from this time, together a team. Never switching players; 83.

playing till the end of time itself and you know with her by your side you win always! Love is far from the buzzer put an end to the game it has just started at the first whistle in life. You look at this beautiful soul and all you see is perfection in her from her beautiful blue eyes, to her lovely brown hair; to her gentle, loving hands that are so warm and caring to hold. Even all these exceptional qualities surpass by her kind caring heart and angel soul that adds so much to her beautiful heart! This made you see that she is your angel in waiting. She has no wings yet, but her halo shines so bright that it cast a beautiful ray of love that only you can see. The beauty of this blessed love of yours has shown you have made you see their greatness before you; where it gives you the courage to succeed, from the love of a sweet angel of yours. Love has helped you to see that we all have greatness in us, you need not have to leap over tall buildings as Superman, or climb on walls of buildings as Spider-man, or even be Sir Lancelot rescuing your Guinevere to be exceptional, just be a kind, loving soul who helps all who are in need, just from saying hi to a stranger. Kindness shows them hey your important enough for someone to take time out of their busy life to say hi. There are many things that one can do to achieve greatness. These qualities are what learned is one that I will never forget! I learned all things are achievable in our life if one is willing to open your heart to others. I love my angel so much. I want nothing more to hold her warm, loving, gentle hands that are the most beautiful to feel and look her in her loving eyes; touch my heart and tell her and to all who reads this I Love this angel with all my heart forever and ever! Love just for one is a gift from God who shows one an angel here on this Earth that is paradise.

Love of an Angel

There comes in one's time of life you find a true love that you know you are destined to be together for all eternity! You find out when you first met that it was fate that brought you both together. Angel is a woman who is the most beautiful soul you have ever seen! Your love goes deeper than physical attraction; it is so deep in your heart that you just know this angel is the one you will be with for eternity! Your love you share is so special; that every time you are near this beautiful angel your heart start to raging a battle. You do not care if you win or lose; because this sweet angel is in your thoughts always! This dear one's power is so great, it makes her the greatest of all angels! When you see her and all you see is the dearest caring soul who has come down from heaven to you! When hearing your heart, it is a beautiful music of love dancing in the sky itself! She has no wings now, because you know all angels do not have wings to be able to soar. One surely has flown into your heart and her halo shows her beauty like no other! She has so much, all that sees her is in awe in the presence that was bestow to them by the good Lord himself. You look at a blessed angel you love so much; all one see, one day you will be with her always! You know in this sea of life, here on this earth, you will always love this dear angel with all your heart! Your angel shares these sweet loving feelings for you. You know that this is the grand lady of your life;

88.

that you have been waiting for. There are many who may say these are foolish thoughts for this time on earth, just see this as a guy who is just being foolish here. I do not see this; it is a love that was destined to be! Because, when two people love each other with all their hearts how can this be foolish! If more people would care instead of hating, this then would be a real paradise for us all.

Magic of Love

There are such great feats of wonders in the night that beckon to be seeing. You can see its glow plainly as one sees stars dancing in the heavens. There are no limits to the power that are so blessed in all who is captivated by it. This beautiful works of wonder is that of love. Everyone has seen its magic at work. We know it, so moves this blessed works of wonder anyone who has ever had their heart held by one who cast magic at then! There is no mirror or Illusion cast; only magic is one that you feel when your heart is beating for your great love! Angel shows you real magic which is a beauty of all you see because she holds you so spellbound in her dear beautiful cast of love. You see this angel as the most beautiful ever in your life! This precious caring soul has shown you such incredible magic in your life; that you will never forget. The blessed spell that she shares with you is one of the sunshine in your life, always, even on the cloudiest of days. It gives you warm feelings of love and eternal happiness which it never sets. You see the beauty of all things of your life now that this dear one is on center stage. You know it will be a call to eternal happiness and love with this beautiful soul of magic! She never makes you feel sad only feel loved; as you make her feel your love always in all you do in your life. One never thinks this magic will bless them, it just happens and when it does, you honestly see what is so beautiful in life. This love is not what all see, but for those who see the real magic of love!

Magic of the moon

The brave warrior of the night is looking for such a magical thing that will give him great power over all who comes near him. It has no limits; it affects all who has been in its power! This is the power of the moonlight that on the darkest of nights; when it rays cast will give others the sense of madness and for others, it is a warm, loving feeling that when a fair maiden becomes to it. She will fall so desperate in love with her noble warrior. This is the power the brave warrior is looking for always. He wants to have such wanting desire of passion that he wants to have and at the same time he wants the power of a true warrior to be able to defeat all his enemies with a gesture, or a swing of his *sword, he knows this magic of the moon is real. He would look for all time to come. The real power of the moon is the passion of love. He has never felt this feeling until recently. This warrior felt his desire come to life on a moonlit night when he spotted the most beautiful maiden of all time! The beautiful fair warrior maiden felt her passion come to life that same night, when she saw her hero in the moonlight and seen his muscles ripple when he ?ex them to her delight. They both then knew the real magic of the moon! The Warrior and his passion of desire made the actual magic of the moon until the sun came up and they lay together so lovingly to watch the sunrise over the treetops meet them a new day to come once more for lovers that are one in all magic of life.* 94.

Mustang

The beautiful mustang runs like the gentle wind blowing ever so active in life that it is meant to be free by God, so beautiful in nature, as surely as the sun dances in the sky. The majestic mustang shows the light to all, who sees this noble of beauty. This beautiful animal is all that symbolize that is pristine and full of life in this world, it shows the strength of nature and beauty so well, you see the muscles of their great legs rippling poise and grace in them it is. This Grace that also is their determination to survive here in nature because, we, man, never learn that we are one with nature, not the master of it. We are just one of many who has the right to live as we see it. So why must we try to own another creature who deserve their Freedom as surely we do. They show the beauty of nature in all its glory. Here so we must accept that we are not the owner of this beautiful planet, just the renter! God is the owner and wants all his tenants to be happy and get along with each other when we learn this will be a real paradise of love, in harmony for us. All who sees these beautiful animals in nature will know the blessed Spirit of grace is nobility always!

My Hero

There are many people we meet in our life that a classed as the hero in our life. The one I look up to is my Dad and he is a caring, loving man who has a dear heart that would help anyone in need. He has sacrificed so much in his life for his family to make sure he provides for them in life. He works hard in his life to creating beautiful things out of wood for others, which he has shown me; the values of hard, honest work for a dollar and being proud of what you do! This shown me that honesty is the best virtue in life; though, he wears no costume with a cape and cannot leap buildings in a single bound, my dad is my hero. He has shown me so much love in my life and helped me see beauty in all things, which resides in all of us in our life; though he works hard, he always seems to have time for his family. He never raised his voice in anger to me when I did something, I should not have done. He took me aside told me what my actions did and let me decide the right thing to do; he never tried to set me on a road I did not want to be. He is far stronger than even mightiest Gods in heart and soul! He never let his family see his sorrow in his life, yet, he did have them, one which I will never forget, the day his beloved went to all Father in Heaven. That Day he showed to me that real love he had with his heart! I feel for him always. He is my dad, who has taught me all I know in my life and the greatest thing is never give up when life gets you down, or when you think the road you are on is a dead end. You just need to find a detour that works in your Life. He is my cowboy with the white hat that will always find me to get for what is right and will never wrong anyone in his life, will give someone something if you are hungry. My dad taught me all I know in the Love of his craft and his kind gentle ways. Some people look up to a comic book character, as the hero, or even some movie actor, plus someone in history, as who are heroes. They may be in life as you know it, but they never will know what my dad knows. They do not have his soul of a dear sweet father. My dad is so kindhearted and such blessed friend to all who knows him. He is all that and then more to me. Even today I can say, even when I am older, I wants to be like him, because my father, who I love so much, is my hero now and forever in my life!

100.

Path of Two Hearts

Everyone has a path that they follows in their life, it is a path of true love. It starts on the road when two people meet on this life journey, they, by chance, or in fact by fate see each other from across a room, or meeting on the street. As walking on a busy sidewalk, or even when two souls by fate meet, even across the distance, through the wonders of computers. I know, you say: how can one fall in love without being close to each other? This is what I call true love, because this shows one's heart so beautifully in this life. You see their soul so well because, you cannot hide what´s in your heart. This path of two hearts has many Looks for all who has taken it, or are still on the road looking for an end to it.

101.

We all will embark on this journey in our lives, and when you find in your heart, you will know she is the one for you! Some search their entire life on this path hoping to bring this journey to an end, yet others think the way is always to search. But after time; you are tired of this ride and want find eternal joy and love with someone who is so special that you want to be with them forever! This heart is so unique to you that she is the one you think of often throughout your day! You want her always to feel loved and be happy. This happy heart is the one you know is the one our lord sent to you! She is so sweet and caring. You see her, show this to you each day; to your heart and to others she has contact. You love everything about this beautiful heart, like her smile that melts you completely; each time she does your breath gets taken away! You get goose bumps when she looks at you with her stunning blue eyes. You see into her eyes and get lost in her pure beauty of her heart that is an angel! Who you know is the one God has sent to you! Before this journey started, you felt as something was missing your life until you met her because, you knew this is the one who would be in your heart always! This love that is so special; because this one of two people who felt unsure of their future, then when they meet and see each other, you just know that your blessed hearts are looking at a future that is beautifully bright. This is a love where you are thinking of

103.

them always! You see this heart and see an angel standing before you, though she has no wings, yet her halo will shine its light on you always! She inspires you so much sense your journey is coming to an end you look at her and see beauty beyond any. You see the beauty of her heart so sweet; which is what set your heart beating only for her! You saw it many times from things she has done, or say to you or, others as this adds so much to her physical beauty a thousand times over! One might say how this love can be so genuine and complete in this life; I say it is a love of not lust, or desire, it is a love of two souls who meet on the path of life.

104.

Rainbow

There are colors of beauty in a rainbow that reflects the love of God himself. God shines us all in our life; it colors is the beauty of one's soul. The beautiful glow of life is rain that makes all things grow, even us all. It shows the beauty of life! The colors of a rainbow is a bridge to heaven, so beautiful, so vast in its glory because, it has no beginning and no ending as it stretches out like a seamless array of the beautiful majesty of life! It is like one could reach out and touch God himself. He is an artist like no other in this life, his masterpieces we see every day, yet, his most priceless wander is one the one only sees if on occasion, because of this, his most prize work so magical in life. You see its glory that we *marvel at that makes all your troubles leaves; this is the blessing of us all! We are truly blessed by this, a view of a great masterpiece a rainbow color of life its self!*

106.

Reflections of One's Soul

One says that you can tell one's heart and soul by the people around them, it is the life of beautiful blessings it is all from the souls of angels that has come to be. It is friends who have given us the beauty of life as we know it! They show us the beauty of all that has been bestowed upon them that God has put in their hearts as the soul of angels that fly towards us each day; that sheds their grace on us always! They are friends who are our angels that God has sent to us to help guide us in our life. Our friends who give us purpose in life. They are the reflection of all that is sweet and caring in this life! You see the blessings they bestowed upon us each day with love from the heart. They are *your angels that have truly ?own into your heart! They have no wings in this Life, yet surely their halos shine like a beacon in the night casting the glow of love and kindness to you and others .You see this many times if we just have the wisdom to see this. They will see it, the blessing of the good Lord that brought you together. He knows that you need an angel in your life to show you the beauty of all his creation in your life. Our Lord Savior's power of love is such beautiful thing to be in, this is wonderful in life when you meet angels who are your friends; that shown you that your soul is a reflection of what you have received. This is a great gift from all who you meet in your life. They are a part of you as surely as your heart beats and gives you life!*

108.

Rose

This beautiful flower adds so much beauty to all that sees it; it petals are shaped so gently on a perfect bud like the love a person holds in your heart for that one blessed loving angel who you know is the love of your life! You find yourself wanting to be, this woman of your dreams always! All you see is the beauty of her heart and soul always. This is far more important than what a person sees in appearance. You see the beauty of her blessed kindness to others and so gentle ways she presents of her! To all, she has the pleasure of knowing! This quality you see in the love of your life, touches all because this is what makes this love so strong, towards your angel. This excellent quality in her adds so much to her breathtaking looks, like no other before you in your life; as a thousand stars add to the vast sky of our universe! You see great beauty in her as of the perfect rose she is. Her soft, gentle hands that you are longing to hold so beautifully shape like petals of rose and to hold them so gingerly. You look at her in her beautiful blue eyes that are like looking at the blue horizon. You lose your thoughts for a moment; because the beauty standing before you moves one completely. When you train your thoughts on what you want to tell her, which is, that she is the most beautiful loving woman of all time; that you and she are in love. You both were fated to find each other and to fall in love. You know you were destining to be together forever! Your angel's beauty is like no other woman you have seen before. You see grace, an eloquent pose where she stands. Her hair is such beautiful strands brown like grains of sand from your heart that your love is ?owing freely for this loving angel before you! The very first moment you heard her beautiful voice for the first time; it is like hearing a beautiful bird singing on a warm spring day, so sweet and so full of wonderful love. You feel for her always standing there and seeing this amazing woman who is your sweet lovely rose. You know she is your soul mate! You know you will be with her forever. You will always be sure, she knows that your love for this dear sweetheart of woman will always be!

111.

Song of My Heart

There is a beautiful melody that beats in us all; that is the song of love. This melody is ever so lovely in this life; one where their music is so beautiful as that of a beautiful songbird singing its beauty of a brand new spring day; after a long winter's nap, where we all are born again to this Blessed day! This is ever so beautiful as the one dear love that has your heart. You feel it deeply as one who has been by God himself, which you have; this lovely beloved princess that you have to see is such blessed dear soul! This angel is the one that you see in your future for all eternity as one looks in the vast heavens of the night sky! You see all the great numbers of stars out there that behold the beauty before you. There is no room in the universe to hold the song in your heart for my love of the beautiful singer in my life! Her melody she sings to my soul is as beautiful as one hears a song that touches your heart. You know not why you love but, this song of love is one of pure beauty to all to hear. You want all to know that you are in love with the most wonderful loving soul you have ever met! This blessed Angel has shown you many beautiful things; that sings from her heart for all time always in perfect pitch never a wrong note sung! Where she holds the key that sings from your heart always. You see the most beautiful of all! This beautiful angel will sing to you always with beauty from her heart. You felt this from the moment you lay your eyes on this dearest singer of your heart. She shares her beautiful heart always! When this angel came to you, you thought there would be no song to share with anyone. You feel her deeply in your very soul, like no other woman you have met before. Love is of the heart from the moment of our first hello. Your sweetheart will always be in your life! She will hold my heart in her hands forever! There are many who would say this is desire, or lust but they are wrong. They do not know the real love of the heart. This sweet angel has the key to my heart always! This beautiful dear angel who sings to my heart is my dear love now and forever! She is my life, my love and my future. This angel will forever have a song in my heart!

114.

Soul of the Hammer

Hammer was sitting there waiting to do what he does best, to add joy, laughter, and peace to all who stands at his vast deeds that gives aspects in his beautiful sounds that ring throughout in the empty void of a shell! There is no heart in it until you hear what makes him ring, the sounds of joy in all! Those who see his beauty are amazed by his deed. There are vast souls out there. You may say a hammer does not have a soul; you would be wrong in this. The hammer has a soul surely as you are standing to gaze at all he has done in his life! If there were no hammer, where would you spend your nights, when it is cold and damp. As the icy wind, on a winter's new dawn day. Then, who bring life to a simple piece of

115.

wood that is just a shell of what is there, would be no marvelous structures for one to gaze and marvel upon! The Hammer would have no soul. The ones who have the heart of the wood to make these things looks beautiful as a sunny summer day where watching the beauty surround you. There are many hammers of different types, as there are many different souls of them. The tool of life that works in metal that drums down a ring that sounds like a church bell on a beautiful Sunday morning! The one who is a wood creator brings to life, the soul of the timber. Those who do not know the essence of the hammer will surely never see the beauty! Wood is never far behind the hammer .They always showing their great teamwork for all to *see his deeds in life! There is a soul of a divine person who holds the tool to bring life. The heart of the creator envisions many great things great things. He can build wondrous things for all to see with hammer's help! There are those who do not see, or understand this. They are not aware that this simple hammer which can drive nails, or pound on metal to make beautiful things can be so much alive in the hands of a craftsman. There is so much more. You then, will see the soul of the hammer!*

Soul of Love

Once in someone's life you come across a person you have a particular connection with that it feels you have known this person your whole life! You love how her heart is so sweet and loving to all she meets; this sets her soul that of a real angel! You want to spend your life with her. She has such a way that brings the best out of people. She inspires all with her loving kindness that adds so much beauty to your life and you cannot help, but fall in love when she shares that love back with you a magic that needs no explanation to you. This is something you just know that was to be! All you think of is the sweet loving woman who has captured your heart dearly, for all time. You know this is a love that fate has brought together! You will always be there for this beautiful soul of a woman that is a gift sent by God. Who knew, this a love of the century and that this man and woman, who will be together and live the dream of happiness and all will see a love of a lifetime that no one will ever tear apart!

Spirit of Love

You come across in time and space a love that is so deep and wonderful in the vast reaches of your heart! It spans the very heavens for all to see and hear. This blessed dear woman who has forever changed your life to a place of true magic that will always cast a spell of beauty from her heart! You feel her spirit in you, always, as surely as one feels the sun on your face on a sweet loving summer's day; this blessed dear soul is one who has to reach your heart when you thought all was not good in life! This angel of your heart has ? own from the heavens to soar her beauty of love to you always, especially when this love is so deep and real in one's life. You feel them in your heart always!

120.

Feelings like this are one of deep loving commitment of the heart that does not spark of desire, but that of true love in one's life. This loving woman who sees your heart, that, of real feelings of yours. You want to spend your life with this dear one, to see her grow old with you. You want to tell this angel I love you. These words are not something found in a book just to say so, but always are from the heart! One who is forever in this blessed love wants their dear one to be happy and when they are in pain, or feeling blue you would gladly take all their hurt away! This dear one has forever blessed your life! She has shown you such beauty of her heart; that has made you see what it is that is crucial in life. You need no material things of the way of man for complete happiness. It is ways of one's heart that bring you joy in your life! The spirit of love is alive in us all, haunting our lives forever which is not scary as a haunted house; it is a spirit we all should learn to embrace! We all need to love more in life, if not this would be pain and suffering in all we do, or say, we all need to bring forth this blessed spirit always!

Spirit of the Wolf

The Wolf is such a beautiful animal here on this Earth. They have such tremendous power in the way they can take down an opponent that is larger than them. Wolves are the great spirit of all animals in how they are; they are so majestic in the way they survive in their way of life. They never kill unless they need to survive for food, or to defend themselves against their pack. There is beauty in the way they move in the way of nature. There is a beauty of nature itself. They move with great stealth; besides stamina that their opponent does not know they are stalking. They are such beautiful animals their fur is an art of nature showing the beauty of their spirits to us. I know some may see these

magnificent animals as horrible when they kill other animals to survive, though we must not fear them, but learn from what they can teach us. These graceful, beautiful acts of nature are our teachers in the way to survive our nature of living. I say we all are one with nature. We are the keepers of the blessed mother Earth. She is one with us all! This beautiful wolf is the spirit we must embrace not fear and the way of her beauty is one with us all! She goes hand and hand with our Savior Jesus Christ that loves us all! His love is in each of us. He showed us that all his creations have great things we can learn from here in this Life! The Spirit of the wolf is strong, loyal, brave, yet beautiful. These qualities we all could use in our hearts; surely when this spirit fades away, we can never see that again. Everyone and everything has a place in this cosmos of the universe, never fear what you do not know in this life. You must embrace it because all you ever lose when you fear is lessons of natures' beauty.

The Greatest Power

There is a power so great out there that no force of nature can make you yield to their strength. You need not have a train for it, or buy it, no amount of gold, or precious gems here on this earth can give you this power; we each have it in our hearts and soul this power. Our Savior Jesus Christ etched the power of giving, sharing and that into our soul! We have seen this power emerge every day when someone is in crises. You think there is no hope out there, then fate steps in; .someone with a soul of an angel see what has befallen you and tries to help out them who is in need. I am not talking about money which is nice; it is when there is a disaster that happens; that is when you see the soul of angels. A complete stranger goes to that person of need and gives them comfort with just a kind word or hug just so that they know they are loved, so they will feel safe. They rebuild their lives by giving them shelter with no thought at all. This is a far greater power then even a terrible weapon can do! That can do tremendous amount damage to our fellow man, or even to a structure, but can it give hope for brighter future? I say no, it cannot. I have seen this happen many of times in my life and I see people act so courageously in these times of needs! This power has given me the wanting to be better to our fellow man! It is sad some do not look in their heart and soul to see this great power would make this better place for us all.

The Gift of Love

There are many types of Love out there that we are a blessing in our lives. The greatest is that love of our Savior Jesus Christ, he loves us so much, and he never judges us for things that are considered wrong in our lives. He sees the beauty of soul and heart always! He knows there is a great good to us all; we all are angels in his eyes and his children will do him proud in the way of goodness. He has seen this done many times in his everlasting watching of his blessed angels. People saw this happen, too, in their short lives of those of his angels who has the wisdom to see this miracle happen. I am talking about the great gift of a love of helping others if they need it! People do these simple acts of helping someone, are real angels. A father, who takes his time to be with his children. He sees the joy of helping them learn to tie their shoes, or learning to ride a bike for the first time. This brings so much pride to the loving parent to see the happy child grows up. They also give the gift of being there for their parents; who as they getting older finds it more difficult to do the things they did in their youth. For the child to see this saddens them, knowing what they become and that is why the loving child, now a young adult sees that love is all that matters. We need nothing of material value to be happy they see that love is all there. They see the great gift of love is such a blessing when strangers come together in tragedy. The Lords has bestowed upon us to show that all can live together in the house of love that is so beautiful! Where us mere keeper of this great lighthouse of life here on this earth sees that this sea of tranquility is so much more, then this will be the great gift of love for us all!

Key to my Heart

There are many locks in one's life that need a key to open. Like the core that opens to your mind to the vast knowledge that lies inside it; that will get you bounties in your life. There is a good job that will bring wealth and satisfaction in a job well done and it also opens your mind to skills of different nature we all have. Then there is a lock of compassion to others to help, if in need. We all have this great key in life. Some fear what they do not understand of this. There is a lock of seeing the Lord and knowing that he loves all; which is a beautiful thing to see and open up in one's life. They never see that love of our Lord can give

131.

you many wonderful things in your life; with this, all things are beautiful in your life having the Lord in your heart never turns you to the wrong door in your life! There is a lock of one's heart that will open you to the feeling of love. There are many kinds of love in one's heart. I'm talking about love between a man and a woman who wants to spend their lives together. They are best friends, as well, as lovers. This feeling is so deep, that you know from the moment you both met, that this would last a lifetime of togetherness that you will share. You want your true love to be happy always! Never do you want to be apart from her. You see all she has done in her life and are so inspired by these great things! You see the most fabulous woman you have met from all she does, or will do in her life. You know she is a special dear caring angel. You see how other people act with your precious angel; also, you know how others move around this sweet, caring soul of your heart. .You knows she is an angel sent to you from Lord himself, you love her so much! You are amazed that this gorgeous woman you love has feelings of love for you as much as your love for her! You never thought you would find someone who is so beautiful. You just love looking at her pictures, which are so gorgeous; yet, this is not the only thing that adds to what you love about her. This sweet angel moves you each day in the kindness to others and the warm caring ways she gives you this adds so much to here beauty! You love her so much in everything she does. You love the way she smiles at you, with her cute dimples showing, so beautifully at you! You are thankful to the Lord for letting you know such a sweet angel! You give thanks to the Almighty for giving you this moment! You know that this life is so blessed now that you're with your soul mate. You know there is more than physical attraction. This love is one of two hearts joining for all time that is beating love for each other by the spirit of two souls that share the same needs in life. They are together now and always; because the key to my heart has been unlocking by angel love of my life.

134.

Tree

There is nothing lovelier than a tree that can breed so much grace and love to one's heart! The tree is the giving soul of life. Which is the beauty of life that is majestic, as there it stands proudly to show such marvelous display where they stand. Trees show great strength in their shape. They can stand to the strongest wind, never giving into this as this it is the way of saying: hey, I am the strength of the Lord! They provide relief of the happening of the daily activities from the scorching sun. They give comfort with shade to giving all life by breathing. The blood of all life that needs it to survive. They are the life vessel of this planet without trees we would not even be here! When their life is over it *is not the end of their Story, because we create things from wood. To breed a new life into them by making things so magical like trees are living again each time you here scrape of hand plane to a roar of a power tool! We give homage and respect for which is most precious the tree, where would we be without them!*

Voice of Love

There is a sound of love beating genuinely inside you. You hear it clearly as one hears a church bell ringing on a quiet Sunday morning with happy children singing the praise of our Lord, who has saved us all! This voice in depths of your heart and soul, when you first laid your eyes on the most beautiful loving woman, you have ever met in your life! This dear angel is such caring woman who you knew from the ? First hello that you shared would be the start of a long beautiful relationship! You need no other in your life because you feel in your heart that this sweet angel of a woman is the one you have been waiting for all your life! She is more beautiful than even a dozen red roses waiting to show *their blooms on Valentine's Day. Her radiant beauty shows so beautifully as the moon shines it beams of love on a clear night sky for all to see. This angel is such shining star that has captured my heart for those to see it beating only for her. This is a beautiful feeling to have. It shows a great cast of light like a diamond, showing its facets of colors for all to marvel at it. This blessed angel knows you like you know your shadow! This feeling we both share is one of great joy that we both found the one who will always make you feel warm and loved. This is your heaven always in eternal happiness for you and your heart beat. This angel is your voice of love now and forever!*

138.

Two Hearts

The love of two people is a special feeling that is so beautiful this love is so special and blessed were these two who love each other so much. When it is this Love, where you feel you are so blessed and that feels as deeply as you can feel them in your heart! You feel that you both are so in love! You have never been this blessed in your life. You and your angel share such a connection; though you are two hearts. You beat the life of your essence as one. This love, you know, will be one that never fades away. This love is strong and profound you feel each other, even when you are not near one another. It is a love that drew two souls who needed to have

this love of the lifetime. That will never die. This love that is so strong you would do anything for them, you would even sacrifice you for the love of yours if it would allow them more precious time here on this earth! Even death would not keep you away from her. You would be her guardian angel. When you both are no more here on this land; you will be free to soar the heavens together holding one another in arms for all time. This type of love you cannot tell others. It is one so magical and beautiful. They need to feel its joy of it, to see the beauty of it.
You know this, because you saw it. You see your Love who is so beautiful in all ways! This sweet, caring angel has such a dear heart that she shows so well.

140.

Your blessed love has gorgeous precious blue eyes. Especially when she looks at you, it is as if looking into the heart of an angel. You know this to be so because she has saved you from being alone forever. You see the angel who has the key to your heart! One who has unlocked it from the bounds! What you never thought was possible! You never thought such a sweet loving woman who is beautiful in all ways could love you as deeply as you love her! You know this love, you both share will give you a life of great joy and love that will be forever together. The beating of hearts will always be as long as you are beating together in harmony with love nothing is impossible!

Voice of Wood

Wood is a great gift from the good Lord that gives us so much in this great life lessons here on this earth. Its voice sings so clearly, you say wood has a beautiful melody of its own. It shows us much. You hear the beauty of its self. Just look at the wonders of patterns of grains you see in just one single board! One who is not into the ways of wood would just see odd random lines in it nothing but funny wavy lines. To the master of creating things from this huge beautiful piece of wood shows the grains of life of God himself in it. Where wood artist sees the multiple images as the blood that gives us life, there is such beauty in all living things in this life.

Never judge things by looks alone. You need to see the inner beauty that all God's creation have in them. This is one of the lessons the wood master learns and to others this seems so unimportant. The masters wood creator so determines to have patience in one's life and never to rush the art that he is creating. There are some in this life want to rush through this and not enjoy the beauty that handed to them, yet there are some in this life knows, yet do not realize they are learning this great lesson of life. The master of wood has to deal with things that might seem difficult. They learn in this life. Experience, you need to take a different path if the original road is being up a hill, where it is difficult to continue there. He learns to adapt and push

143.

forward. They know the first path may be impossible to stay, so they choose not an easier one, but one that helps them to show the beauty of one's self-worth. That can learn to survive. They show much skill in their craft for making beautiful joints that, to a person not knowing of wood, thought dif?cult [difficult] to do, where the one of wood need always to learn and perfect what you do. This lesson is right in all things of this life. Then the greatest lesson of all in this life is to be at peace in harmony with one's self with others! If everyone follows these lessons, this earth could be a real paradise. We are forever in debt to the greatest teacher who has shown us the blessed lessons of wood the beautiful soul of this place we call home!

144.

Window to your Heart

There comes a time in one's life and you meet a loving soul that apparently changes your outlook on life. You do not know how this happens. This opens your heart like a window into your soul. As this feeling is a view that will forever change your life that one never thought that you find in someone you want to spend your life with forever. This loving heart is the most beautiful loving caring angel you have ever met in your entire life. Your window to your soul was one that was never clear, as it is with this loving angel! You knew she was special, even when you first met her. This dear angel has shown you a whole new outlook on your life that shows you had potential in you, never knew existed before meeting the one you call your one true love. This beautiful woman has the heart of an angel. That cares for you so deeply which you know will be this way always! You see the love she has given you and it touches you always. She is your inspiration in all you do in this life. You see the beauty of her heart and soul. This blessed angel has a way that makes all you want to better them. The caring she gives to others is so exquisite this it is what makes this dear heart of yours so truly unique! You know that you both are two beats in a heart; that beats a rhythm for each other. You both love one another with all your heart! This loving angel has shown you many loving and caring things in this sea of life. You look into her beautiful, loving eyes and you see *your future, because this angel is a beautiful life with this dear heart. This is a blessed gift for you both that our Lord has given to you! Your angel has freed your heart from being alone. You will be with her always and will be forever a team in the grand scheme of life doing beautiful things together always. The window of your heart is never as clear as it has been now.*

Wisdom of an Owl

An owl is so wise and majestic in his ways of life; he can see things that no other bird can see. Its sight is like no other before him, this majestic bird of wisdom can see wonders like no other bird can before him. There is such a grander about the wise owl that takes things not for granted and can wait till the time is right to take action, he has the patience to wait until he can move like a breeze in the wind, though he is not the most majestic of the birds of prey, they help the environment like no other of the birds; by taking small rodents for food, which if we did the same it will make our stomach quake. The nobility of birds are well known, because they have a beauty no other have. Owls can

148.

see things in the darkest of nights like no other of Gods most beautiful creations here in this sea of life. It is a shame people do not have the grace or wisdom of the wise owl; just think if we did, no one would be in a rush in this life and learn to enjoy a life that the good Lord has given them, where some see the owls as a small unattractive bird. I see the beauty of them in the way of life and the wisdom they show in their action! They will never dull in their beauty of nature. We would all be better if we had some of their wisdom, to wait before taking action.

Touch by Heart

There is love out there for all to see in one's life that will forever change your life! One who is truly your angel in life and who will never judge you for what you do in your life. This dear angel will always tell you how proud she is of you; when you think you are alone in this world. Your life is a crossroad, not a dead-end in it; just no direction which to go then low beholds a dear sweet, caring soul comes to you! God saw you needed someone as much as they need you. I have found love in this dear angel with this precious, blessed angel, there are no cloudy days. Only days of sunshine that beams such a glow that you see it's sure as you hear a train whistle at the crossing

150.

before you. It is the most beautiful way of life. It's breathtaking as one sees a night sky with stars flickering its brilliant twinkles to you as to say: hey, this beautiful life - enjoy it, this is heaven to us! All stars dance their great dance of life to us even when one thinks there is no hope in life, because when you have someone you love and they love you back, you are touched in the heart that all sees before them this beauty of love everlasting in one eye now and forever!

151.

Shadow of Heart

Life loneliness brings questions to one's heart as to what purpose is there out there for me on this path being traveled here in this world? The cold winter's winds blowing across plains of life have a razor edge that inevitably cuts like as a knife. The bleeding of one's soul feels the draining of happiness that wants to heal by knowing love sought out. God feels your pain across the streaming cosmos and sends one heart who is destined to be the one who is your angel from Heaven that saves you. First time when we met, it was a moment filled with magic that time stood still, because when two are in love, there is nothing more important! From this time forward there is no other in my heart beating the everlasting we share and the beauty we see out there is truly breathtaking! The birds sing our song in the hours we are living and the beautiful sun warms us dearly with rays of love, we are embracing in our hearts. As from the moment in time, our hearts are one. The light, the beautiful light shining beautifully with a cast I see standing by me, because this dear one who I love is my shadow of my heart that will stand with me always! We are two hearts, always joined in all life we are living here in time and space.

A Son's Love

The beating of a heart, my heart that sings of a harmony deep inside who touches me dearly in my days that I am living who brought life to me. The age of the hours standing forth me with the wisdom of time is one man who I call my father who I love dearly in my heart. His knowledge he shares freely I hold dearly with pride and love that never will fade away like a rose withering in time. Seasons comes with changing pictures in the moments we are sharing that takes one's breath away by the pure beauty of us that at times we forget. Time has a way to flow the ever-shifting sands we are traveling in life's roads that make the journey rough with hazards that cause one hurt with an ache cause us to wonder. What there is there~~fore~~ *for* us and leave us a feeling that makes it seem we are alone with no one to share your life joys and misery, but never forget that you never feel that you are because when one has a family, you are not. You always loved by all and especially by me, who shares a son's love that is no passing in times moments but is for today, tomorrow, and for all days is for you always!

155.

Dearest Dad

My Dearest Dad,
My heart is aching from the hurt you are going through that brings you much pain that you do not deserve. The memories appear in my of our past that we shared of joys and sorrows, where you were my anchor in saying no matter what comes there is a tomorrow: when you believe in the life beautiful, and you held me in your loving arms. I look back over the years to see your great strengths you shown from your great skill to make things of beauty that moves those around you by what created from you dear caring hands. Dad, you always made time for me in what I needed and shared your knowledge of life that I hold dearly in my heart, my beating heart that I share with those who needs help. My heart aches in the hurt you endured in our life, where you never complain or shed a tear except the day your dear love,

Mom was called to God. Which hurts me so much seeing you with so much sadness like I am feeling right now when you called to our Lord Savior Jesus Christ. But I know you can once again be with your beautiful love, my Mom and can be happy. As this all, I ever wanted to you and our family who I love dearly in my heart! I hope you know how much I love you and can be proud of me in what I do for our family that means so much to me. I keep seeing little things that remind me of you and know though you are not here with us now that you are not far because I carry your love deep in my heart! I know time will ease my painful loss though I want to let you know I will never forget you and will never let your memory fade away! Dad please know you always loved by our family and me and you will never be forgotten because as long as we live you will live: as we are your legacy that will hold dearly in our hearts that loves you so much! Take care my dearest Dad and from time to time come by to say hello as we welcome you always and we continue living. Though it will be rough at times, we can make because you were our teacher and Dad who taught us well who we will love always!

Love your son Robert

Susan,

May the light of the lord always shine on you on the road of life that shines love in your heart

Robert Macke

CPSIA information can be obtained
at www.ICGtesting.com
Printed in the USA
LVOW12s1411080518
576428LV00001BA/25/P

9 781387 290857